HERBERT YPMA

HIP
HOTELS
LONDON

with 277 illustrations, 233 in color

Thames & Hudson

contents

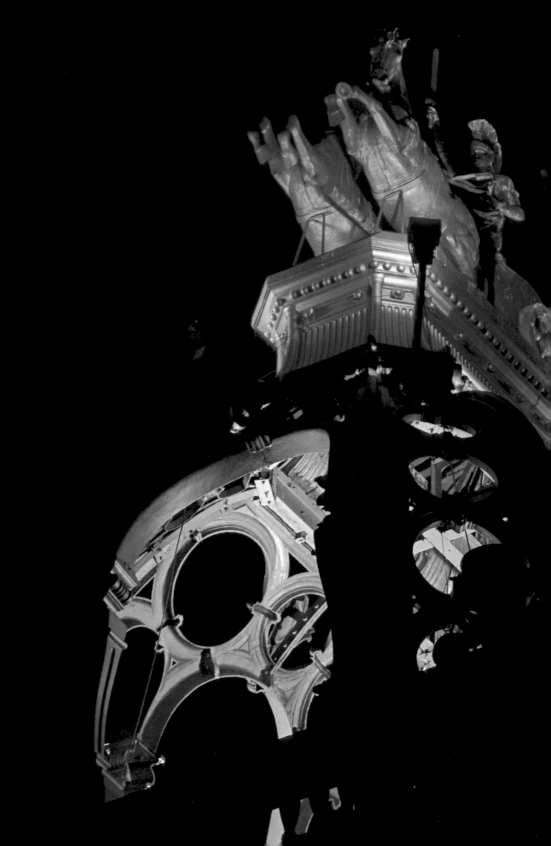

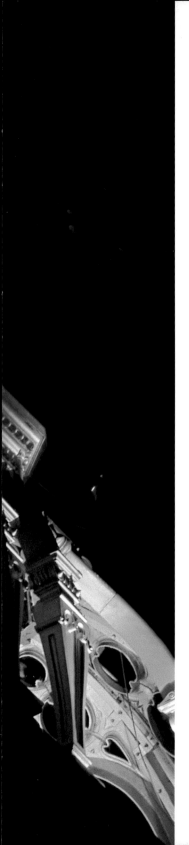

what is HIP?

Travel has changed. No corner of the world is unfamiliar anymore; globetrotting has become decidedly more democratic; cut-price air fares make almost any destination possible; and the easing of border bureaucracy has undoubtedly made things less of a hurdle.

What this means is that we are now free to pursue experiences on a more individual level; to seek out destinations that strike a personal note in terms of architecture, location, ambience and design – destinations that make us think, 'Now that's my kind of place.'

And that, from the very beginning, has been the point of HIP HOTELS; to find and share unique, authentic, inspiring places that will make you simply want to 'pack a bag and go'. And you can go secure in the knowledge that there have been no short-cuts taken. Each hotel featured is one that I have stayed in myself and photographed. That's your assurance and guarantee that all the hotels in this book are truly **H**ighly **I**ndividual **P**laces.

Herbert Ypma

introduction

Divided into thirty-one boroughs, each with a population of between 150,000 and 300,000 residents (8 million in total), stretching for 30 miles at its widest point, London is in all respects the largest city in Europe. Ethnically speaking, it is probably also the most diverse.

But it is neither its size nor its diversity that makes it such a magnet. Rather it is its dynamic as a centre of a liberating, democratic mindset that has for centuries attracted free thinkers of their time. Whether in literature, music, art, fashion or even politics, England's capital has long hosted those interested in variety, controversial or otherwise. George Frederick Handel, Karl Marx, Anna Pavlova, Arthur Rimbaud, Piet Mondrian, Oscar Wilde and Sigmund Freud, to name but a few, all left their mother country to revel in the freedom Britain offered and in its willingness to broadcast, and not just tolerate, bold new ideas.

London does not have Rome's wealth of antiquity, nor does it share Paris's beautifully uniform architecture. It's a higgledy-piggledy mix of buildings and building styles spread over such a distance that exploration on foot is next to impossible, not to mention the unsuitability of the roads for flitting around. Yet, more so than any other city on the planet, London is a powerfully interesting place, largely because its citizens are interested.

Any artist, whether he writes, paints, acts, composes, dances, designs or stands on a soapbox, needs an audience, and the more informed and open the audience the greater the incentive for the artist. Londoners know the magic formula: anything goes – from crusty gentleman's club to punk rock – as long as it's not boring, stupid or obvious.

chelsea

Mini skirts, long hair, bell bottoms, big sunglasses, lots of drugs and way too much use of the word 'groovy': Chelsea virtually invented the sixties. King's Road was an address known the world over and people identified it with Mary Quant, the Rolling Stones, Lulu, Jimi Hendrix, Donovan and the 'fifth Beatle' George Best, etc. Britannia was cool and Chelsea was the source.

As it turned out, the party was over by the time the next decade started. British tax laws chased the home-grown stars away and those in the 'art scene' became disillusioned, cashed in their overvalued studios and moved to Devon and Cornwall.

Today Chelsea is distinguished more by luxe than by cool. It has morphed into one of London's most desirable and expensive residential areas, yet somehow it has miraculously managed to retain the atmosphere of a village – a slightly bohemian, urban village. The residents

may be bankers and stockbrokers but they're doggedly resisting a slippers-and-flannel-pyjamas lifestyle in favour of a cappuccino-and-designer-label alternative. People live in small cottages, elegant terraces and converted stables instead of large mansions, and yet they miss nothing because there is so much to see and do on their doorstep.

Neighbouring Knightsbridge and South Kensington offer great shopping and high culture. Harrods and its edgier alternative Harvey Nichols have to form the core attraction in the retail sense. Just a bit further along is the V&A, the world's most comprehensive museum dedicated to the decorative arts. Add the Natural History Museum, the Royal Geographic Society and the Albert Hall, as well as the boutiques of Walton Street, Sloane Street and Brompton Cross, and you can grasp why real estate prices are not about to come down any time soon.

myhotel chelsea

Tucked into a quiet little street just behind Brompton Cross – a chic corner of town that is dense with fashionable shops, restaurants and cafés – myhotel Chelsea has undoubtedly the best location in the area. Chanel, Paul Smith, Ralph Lauren, Jean-Paul Gaultier and Nicole Farhi are just around the corner, as are the Joseph flagship stores for men and women. Bibendum, Terence Conran's first and probably most successful combination of design and haute cuisine, is strategically situated in the original Conran shop; also nestled between designer boutiques is Daphne's, another classic London restaurant. Then there's Walton Street, a charming little row of tiny terraced houses offering an eclectic array of one-off ventures, such as an antique shop stocked only with must-have pieces for men. Other local hotspots include innovative sushi restaurants like Itsu and cocktail bars like Bardo. Add London's most exclusive gym – KX – and you get an idea of why people who stay at myhotel Chelsea find it difficult to go anywhere else.

But the appeal is not just in the location. Architect and proprietor Andy Thrasyvoulou, known to his staff as Mr T, has created something new in London – a small, club-like hotel that does not subscribe to any club clichés. One guest perhaps managed to sum it up best when he described the hotel as 'refreshingly bright'. And that's the difference. Darkness is a bit of a London signature – dark nicotine-stained pubs, dark leather Chesterfields, sombre colours, even entire rows of houses, such as those in historic Bedford Square, painted black. But, as England's northern European neighbours have long understood, having as much light as possible simply makes you feel better.

my hotel

chelsea

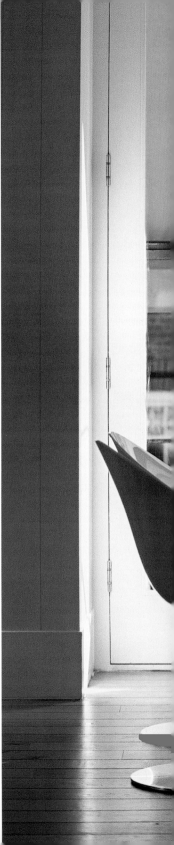

There are many smaller hotels in London that are charming and cosy and comfortable, but not many are airy and light. Add big bathrooms, down pillows, Thai silk comforters, flatscreen TVs, DVD players and all the cyber-communication ports you could possibly want, and you start to get the picture. myhotel Chelsea is the embodiment of New London: modern, hip, contemporary, but not at the expense of comfort, and not by sacrificing the Englishness that makes London so appealing.

address myhotel Chelsea, 35 Ixworth Place, London SW3 3QX
tel (44) (0)20 7225 7500 **fax** (44) (0)20 7225 7555
e-mail chelsea@myhotels.com
room rates from £250

absolutely have to see
The Victoria & Albert Museum, Cromwell Road, London SW7 2RL (tel 7942 2000): the world's greatest museum dedicated to the decorative arts; where else will you see an intact Frank Lloyd Wright interior?

must have lunch
The Oyster Bar at Bibendum, Michelin Building, 81 Fulham Road, London SW3 6RD (tel 7581 5817): cold seafood in an old tyre HQ? Surprise yourself!

blakes

Painted a completely unexpected shade of dark, dark, British racing green, this row of terraced houses in Roland Gardens hints unambiguously that here is anything but convention at play. Blakes is clearly not for people who like the safe and the predictable. While the favourite colour for local interiors is over-whelmingly magnolia – an almost ubiquitous version of a creamy off-white – Blakes's interiors revel in deep, rich shades of navy blue, black, terracotta and brown.

With the discerning taste of an antiquarian and the refined eye of a couturier, Lady Anouska Weinberg (the creative talent and motivating force behind the hotel) has put her unique stamp on an environment that mixes the exotic allure of an Oriental opium den with the casual, aristocratic-style, deep-buttoned comfort of a British club.

Thai silk, Venetian mirrors, Chinese antiques, blue and white porcelain, delicate birdcages, old books, elaborately framed architectural drawings, Biedermeier dressers, Empire beds and countless faux bamboo lamps constitute a decorative signature that is unlike anything you're likely to find anywhere else. And that's the enduring charm of Blakes: it has a look all of its own, which, together with the help of an excellent kitchen and fine-tuned professional staff, translates into an experience that's completely individual.

Even though Blakes is now into its third decade, it never fails to impress. Guests who already know the hotel are reminded of its fearless flair, while newcomers are bewitched by its romantic aura. But there is something really clever about Blakes – something you don't see – and this no doubt is the key to its timeless status.

Despite the initial impression of a hotel that is unbridled in its eclectic eccentricity, the Blakes environment is actually a result of very careful consideration, painstaking attention to detail and rigorous discipline in terms of selecting the right piece for the right room. As with most things, what appears to be effortless and natural in fact involves an extraordinary amount of effort.

Blakes is a truly London experience. You would not find this hotel in any other city. In an age of increasing internationalism in terms of design and decoration, keeping something specific to London is not only worthwhile but absolutely essential to the experience of travel. An indication of the hotel's success tends to be seen at breakfast-time. The first thing guests comment on is how impressed they are with their room. No wonder, then, that at a recent industry awards evening, Blakes carried away the 'Test of Time' trophy.

address Blakes Hotel, 33 Roland Gardens, London SW7 3PF
tel (44) (0)20 7370 6701 **fax** (44) (0)20 7373 0442
e-mail blakes@blakeshotels.com
room rates from £175

absolutely have to see
The Buddhist Pavilion in nearby Battersea Park: crossing the Thames over the Albert Bridge completes the experience

must have lunch
Star of India, 154 Old Brompton Road, London SW5 0BE (tel 7373 2901): sophisticated cuisine from India in an Italianate neoclassical interior; a hip mix

notting hill & bayswater

London, for Londoners, is defined by the river (the Thames) and the park (Hyde Park). 'South of the river', 'north of the river', the East End, the West End: orientation is much less formal than the numbered arrondissements of Paris or the grid system of New York, yet everyone knows exactly what is meant, or should that be exactly *where* is meant.

'North of the park' means Notting Hill and Bayswater. Since the eponymous film starring Hugh Grant and Julia Roberts came out, Notting Hill has no doubt officially usurped Chelsea's long-lost crown in terms of hip street cred and funky lifestyle. With its bars, clubs, one-off boutiques, summer street carnival and the hugely popular bric-à-brac eccentricity of Portobello Market, it's hard to believe that this area was, until fairly recently, one of the most notoriously impoverished in London.

But that, exactly, was its appeal. All the large, run-down, Victorian and Edwardian houses provided a perfect opportunity for artists, film directors and writers to afford the kind of space they aspired to, and slowly Notting Hill gentrified into a Chelsea incarnate, though with a distinct Afro-Caribbean flavour.

Today the price of real estate in Notting Hill suggests that street cred is diminishing in favour of 'City bonus'-boosted consumerism, but the area has an escape valve in the form of nearby Bayswater. Though it has been blessed with acres of elegant Victorian and Edwardian squares, Bayswater still has the slightly run-down ambience so essential to depressed real estate prices.

So, if Notting Hill is the new Chelsea, then it follows that Bayswater might well be the new Notting Hill....

the portobello

For the past three decades the Portobello Hotel has been a true original. In a way it is the granddaddy of Hip Hotels – the original eccentric outsider that kick-started the trend for small, offbeat hotels where the interior design is cutting-edge, staff are attentive but discreet, and lobby and rooms alike are intended to feel as intimate as home: a nesting experience without the drudgery of tidying up.

Established in 1971 by Johnny Ekperigin and designed by Julie Hodges, the Portobello has consistently been one of London's most desirable places to stay. The owners discovered long ago that the key to success was to play up the hotel's quirks and style. This is a place that happily flaunts its own originality. The rooms – unusual, inventive, cosy and very sexy – have that much admired haphazard, casual look that is deemed so typically English; an unlikely mishmash of styles that attracts an equally unlikely mishmash of legendary guests, like the ageing rocker Alice Cooper, who requested regular deliveries of white mice from the local pet shop to feed the boa constrictor that he kept in the bath, or Tina Turner, who fell so much in love with the place that she just had to buy the house next door.

Some of the Portobello's rooms have become as legendary as the guests themselves. Take the room with 'the waterworks', for example, a playboy-hippy-of-the-sixties-style suite equipped with a 'Victorian bathing machine': a marvellously eccentric collection of copper pipes, taps and massive sprinkler, all surgically attached to a turn-of-the-century claw-footed bath, standing in the middle of the room, directly behind a massive round bed tucked into the bay window.

Then there is the 'four-poster room', which contains an Elizabethan bed so high and large that you need a ladder to climb into it. And for those who like to hide in attics there are two fully fledged Moroccan chambers tucked under the roof. Moody, dark and dangerously seductive, their rich reds and layers of carpets and cushions evoke the atmosphere of a Berber tent.

In a democratic spirit, the hotel also includes rooms that are realistically affordable. Plus you're staying in the middle of London's hippest neighbourhood. Whether it's antiques and vintage clothing you're after, or just groceries and people-watching, Notting Hill is a treasure-trove and a parade. All in all staying at the Portobello feels just like spending a few days with a funky old aunt who was once a flower child....

address The Portobello Hotel, 22 Stanley Gardens, London W11 2NG
tel (44) (0)20 7727 2777   **fax** (44) (0)20 7792 9641
e-mail info@portobello-hotel.co.uk
room rates from £130 inc. breakfast

absolutely have to see
Portobello Market, Portobello Road, London W11: a quintessentially English street market famous for its antiques and bric-à-brac; best on a Saturday

must have dinner
Julie's Restaurant and Bar, 135 Portland Road, London W11 4LW (tel 7229 8331): romantic, louche, full of fairy-lit alcoves and nooks and crannies; another magnetic Ekperigin experience

guesthouse west

Notting Hill is the neighbourhood with the most interesting shops, some of the best bars, and – as most residents like to think – the most interesting people. It's as representative of today's London as Chelsea was of the swinging sixties.

Thirty years ago it was a different story. Notting Hill had potential, but mainly because property was so cheap. Though the old Edwardian boxes in the neoclassical Georgian style were arranged in stately fashion along elegantly curving tree-lined streets, the area was a renovator's and bargain-hunter's paradise, and it inevitably attracted the crowd with more imagination than cash. The raw, real style of the area was a plus, as was the local market on Portobello Road, which has since grown into an institution.

Today, though the area has its fair share of high-street names, it is still punctuated with genuine one-offs. Instead of a Sainsbury's or a corner shop you'll find Tom's Deli, a delicatessen-style café that disguises itself as a downmarket grocery store but where a table for Saturday morning brunch is a hard-won prize.

To launch a hotel in the middle of what is now a hyper-hip neighbourhood is obviously a smart move. Guesthouse West is located in a house typical of the area, and it's not clear what to expect from the outside. The proprietors decided against minimalism or faux glamour. Instead they chose a mid-century modern look, with rich, sensual and tactile interiors. The hand-waxed leather furniture is bound to evoke a few 'hey, we used to have a couch like that before my mother gave it to the church'-type comments, but ultimately it's not the individual pieces that distinguish this place so much as the way the different ingredients have been combined.

Each guest room is different, but they are unified by a palette of exotic timber veneers set against white walls. The interiors are neither far out and funky nor predictable and boring. The aesthetic is like the area – different but not outrageously so. In fact the hotel reminds me of the best boutiques in Notting Hill: clean, simple spaces where you can find unusual, unexpected pieces. Guesthouse West whispers originality, it doesn't yell it.

Neither is it a design statement. It's not even particularly pace-setting ... and that's the point. It combines a look that wouldn't be out of place in the pages of *Wallpaper* with the slightly shabby, 'let's not try too hard' style of Notting Hill.

address Guesthouse West, 163–165 Westbourne Grove, London W11 2RS
tel (44) (0)20 7792 9800 **fax** (44) (0)20 7792 9797
e-mail Enquiries@guesthousewest.com
room rates from £145

absolutely have to see
Solange Azagury-Partridge, 187 Westbourne Grove, London W11 2SB
(tel 7792 0197): one of the most original jewelry boutiques in Europe

must have lunch
Tom's Delicatessen, 226 Westbourne Grove, London W11 2RH (tel 7221 8818):
with the Conrans, food and style are obviously in the blood, but the affordability
of Tom Conran's landmark is new

the pavilion

King George III in snakeskin boots; British Regency meets rock 'n' roll; the Raj and the rage.... The Pavilion is the kind of place that tends to conjure up exotic soundbites. Photographers like to shoot here, musicians like to hang out here, and aspiring models and thespians like to make it their London base. So what's the big deal with the Pavilion?

Well, apart from the fact that it's as mad as King George himself, and as funky as Keith Richards before he moved to Connecticut, it's also funny, kinky, weird, psychedelic, sweet, colourful and unexpected. This kind of inspired creativity usually comes at a premium – 'You want style? You've got to pay for it' – but the Pavilion is that rarest of exceptions, a Highly Individual Place at an affordable price.

And all those soundbites come in handy, because to describe the hotel in more formal terms would require many, many pages of prose. Far better to look at the pictures and to read about the passion of the founding proprietor. As is so often the case, the hotel is the direct result of an obsession ... in this case, not for hotels but for collecting.

Noshi Karne freely admits that she can't help herself. She's a flea-market junkie. For years she'd been buying pieces that she had neither the room nor the need for. Storage space after storage space filled up with finds from her excursions to estate sales, garage sales and village fêtes in the British countryside. The hotel was to provide the perfect opportunity for her to empty those storage units. She has used her beloved treasures to decorate the Pavilion's thirty rooms, and the result is a hotel jammed full of quirky personality.

It goes without saying that each room is different. Guests can stay in a Chinese opium den or a red-and-white-striped military campaign tent, a bright pink Indian suite or the Kasbah-themed ground floor. There's no rhyme or reason to any of it. The rooms are the result of pure whimsy. And that's exactly the charm of it. The Pavilion does not pretend to be anything other than a bit of wackiness in downtown London.

Is there no downside, then, to this Bayswater gem? Well, the location is not exactly posh, and the all-in-one fibreglass bathrooms look as if they've been borrowed from a correctional facility. But that aside, I can't think of a place offering better value in London. You'd better get your skates on: stylish bargains in big cities are as rare a sighting as an Asian tiger.

address Pavilion Hotel, 34–36 Sussex Gardens, London W2 1UL
tel (44) (0)20 7262 0905 **fax** (44) (0)20 7262 1324
e-mail HOTELPAVILIONUK@aol.com
room rates from £60 inc. breakfast

absolutely have to see
Alfies Antique Market, 13–25 Church Street, London NW8 8DT (tel 7723 6066): treasure trove of antiques and bric-à-brac

must have lunch
The plethora of Lebanese restaurants on nearby Edgware Road

the hempel

We clutter our lives with scores of meaningless possessions. They become a burden and soon we are enslaved to them. Without any possessions, say Zen Buddhists, we can once again be free to enjoy ourselves and our lives. It sounds a reasonable proposition, but only the very, very brave among us would take everything we own to the tip. A more sensible option is to go to the Hempel, for here is a hotel where you can sample 'minimalism'.

Named after London-based design dynamo Anouska Hempel (aka Lady Weinberg, also owner of Blakes), this hotel is cool, white and empty on a monumental scale – a place of real Zen-like simplicity. Created from a row of five perfectly restored Edwardian townhouses just north of Hyde Park, it is the embodiment of the belief that space is the ultimate luxury in a big city.

The lobby, described by *Harpers & Queen* as 'larger than an Olympic-size swimming pool', is entirely paved in oversize squares of classic Portland limestone and distinguished by a series of geometric cutout spaces that admit pools of warm sunlight. At night, it glows with light and warmth from two very long, very low and very horizontal hearths that must rank as the most elegant fireplaces in the world.

The whole interior was conceived according to an Oriental concept of simplicity. 'For ten years I wanted to create this kind of hotel,' explained Hempel. 'It was the result of a desire for radical change.' One room has a floating bed, suspended in the middle of the room like a giant cage; others have a stone bath built into the window recess; in some bathrooms the tap water is illuminated at night by fibre optics.

Even the hotel's garden continues the pared-down, east-west theme. Situated in a traditional square opposite the entrance, it is almost as if every leaf has been styled to Anouska Hempel's exacting standards. Individual teak and brass recliners – the kind that used to be found on old ocean liners – are positioned between ornamental trees and herb-filled borders. Three square pools echo and reflect the formal architecture of the hotel façade. Particularly in summer, the lavender- and rosemary-scented garden adds another dimension to the hotel, not to mention making a fabulous location for breakfast.

The success of the Hempel emphasizes one glaring truth about minimalism: the more you leave out, the better what is left has to be. It is not for the faint-hearted. Less is definitely more – more demanding, more interesting and more exciting.

address The Hempel, 31–35 Craven Hill Gardens, London W2 3EA
tel (44) (0)20 7298 9000   **fax** (44) (0)20 7402 4666
e-mail hotel@the-hempel.co.uk
room rates from £165

absolutely have to see
Electric Cinema, 191 Portobello Road, London W11 2ED (tel 7908 9696):
this old cinema, styled like a theatre, has been given a new lease of life by
hip hangout style master Nick Jones: you can drink and eat while you watch

must have lunch
The Cow, 89 Westbourne Park Road, London W2 5QH (tel 7221 0021): have a
pint and a plate of oysters in an old-style pub specializing in new-style seafood

hyde park

Unlike any other big city, London is distinguished by its grand parks. St James's Park calls to mind the Changing of the Guard and the majesty of the Mall. Regent's Park recalls the imperial grandeur of Edwardian England. Battersea Park, by contrast, evokes the modest optimism of post-war Britain. Yet of all of London's vast green spaces, none is more redolent of the city than Hyde Park.

Even today, Parisians who come to London for the first time start frantically tapping the taxi driver's window when he takes a short cut through the park, convinced that they have somehow wandered into the English countryside. With its carefully considered planning, in the tradition of Great British landscaping, Hyde Park gives the impression of being a vast stretch of pure nature that has somehow managed to avoid an urban fate. As plenty of lively historical anecdotes attest, it is certainly not a park in the constrained, formal sense that we associate with most big cities.

During the Second World War, for instance, Winston Churchill could be found taking his trusty steed for a long, hearty gallop along the riding trails in the early morning mist, fortified by the odd swig of cognac. In the nineteenth century Queen Victoria chose the park as the location for the Crystal Palace, a monumental glasshouse built to house the first World Trade Fair. And a few centuries earlier, Hyde Park was where Sir Christopher Wren built Kensington Palace for the British royal family (Princess Diana was later to be a tenant).

The Serpentine river and lake bisecting the park have remained unchanged since the 1730s, but the Serpentine Gallery has become one of the most distinguished venues for contemporary art and architecture. Seamlessly, effortlessly, Hyde Park remains an integral part of London and is a fine example of the city's unique ability to both sustain continuity and nurture innovation.

baglioni

It was only a matter of time before a hotel would recognize the appeal of this particular stretch of Kensington. Situated directly opposite Hyde Park, diagonally across from Kensington Palace, and a hop, skip and a jump from the Royal Albert Hall, Baglioni may just have nabbed one of London's most promising locations. True, Kensington High Street is all hustle and bustle, but that's how many people prefer it, and if you want total serenity the park is just across the street.

I know this area well. My uncle was with the Dutch embassy and their apartments were a few doors down from Baglioni. As a regular houseguest, I was so spoiled: I thought that taking the dogs for long walks in the park and playing tennis at Queens was normal!

But despite the privilege of Baglioni's location, it has something else going for it. It has the style and service unique to Italian hospitality, bang in the centre of London. The owner, the management and all the staff are Italian, and the service is truly exceptional. Whether it's breakfast in the morning or a drink at the bar, the staff have that way of making you feel as if you're their long-awaited first guest.

Even the design – a rich mix of dark woods, contemporary furniture, vivid silks with velvets, and more than a splash of gold – feels very Italian, though it's not. It's the work of Gil Dez, and how he ended up with the position of in-house designer is a nice story. He was the designer and co-proprietor of the Villa Gallici in Aix-en-Provence – an enchantingly romantic property, and so convincing that the proprietor of the Baglioni wanted to buy it. Flattered, Dez and his partners explained that it wasn't for sale … until they saw the number Roberto Polito had written down.

It was the beginning of a new hotel life for Gil Dez. He came on board as the in-house designer for the Baglioni hotels, and the merger that resulted from this meeting of pure happenstance has produced some emotive results.

Designwise, London's Baglioni is completely different to Aix-en-Provence but what it shares is Dez's attention to detail and a pragmatic, experience-generated feel for what people want in a hotel.

address Baglioni, 60 Hyde Park Gate, London SW7 5BB
tel (44) (0)20 7368 5700   **fax** (44) (0)20 7368 5701
e-mail info@baglionihotels.com
room rates from £210

absolutely have to see
The Serpentine Gallery in the park (tel 7402 6075): especially in summer when a temporary annex is commissioned from a legendary architect (past examples have included Oscar Niemeyer, Daniel Libeskind and Zaha Hadid)

must have lunch or afternoon tea
The Orangery at Kensington Palace (tel 7376 0239): the most – and only – stylish royal thing you can do in London

the metropolitan

What exactly is it that makes the Metropolitan such a scene? According to designer Keith Hobbs, who with partner Linzi Coppick applied a similar formula of refined restraint to the ultra hip Clarence Hotel in Dublin, the aim was to give the Metropolitan a 'buzzy democratic feel'. A cool, calm, airy space is what was envisaged.

A fashion analogy seems inescapable, particularly given the success in the world of retail fashion of its proprietor, Singapore-based Christina Ong. In addition to Donna Karan and Prada concessions, she is the name behind Armani in London. And, appropriately, the Metropolitan is rather like an Armani suit. On the rack it may not look much, but it can do amazing things for the person wearing it. The emphasis is on the quality of the materials and on the elegance of the cut. The same is true of the Metropolitan's interiors. The finest materials – special leathers by Bill Amberg, carpets by Helen Yardley and custom-made furniture such as the dining chairs inspired by Frank Lloyd Wright – combine to create an elegant, understated environment that comes to life with the addition of people.

In today's world, explains Hobbs, 'the most valuable commodity is space, and so we wanted to create an air of space … a determined bid for light and simplicity.' For once, this 'less is more' ethos also follows through to the prices. 'We didn't just want financial high flyers drinking Dom Perignon,' says Hobbs. Rooms are not, by London standards, expensive, and in the extremely fashionable restaurant, Nobu, the average price per person is still well within the budget of most city types. If you can get a table, that is.

Since its opening in 1997, Nobu has consistently remained one of the most sought-after and high-profile establishments in London. A dinner booking is still almost impossible unless booked well in advance, though hotel guests do get to jump the queue.

Nobu is the creation of Japanese master chef Nobuyuki Matsuhisa. Trained as a sushi chef in Tokyo, he travelled throughout South America before eventually establishing a Japanese restaurant in Lima, Peru. His South American experience accounts for his highly inventive food, which mixes Japanese cuisine with South American spices and ideas. And in the restaurant, as throughout the hotel, the design takes a supporting role, allowing the contemporary London lifestyle to be the real focus of attention.

address The Metropolitan, Old Park Lane, London W1K 1LB
tel (44) (0)20 7447 1000 **fax** (44) (0)20 7447 1100
e-mail info.lon@metropolitan.como.bz
room rates from £320

absolutely have to see
The food hall at Harvey Nichols, Knightsbridge, London SW1X 7RJ (tel 7235 5000): see just how hip London can get, with the most humorously inventive packaging in the world

must have lunch or dinner
Downstairs at Nobu (tel 7447 4747): still one of the most popular culinary experiences in London

mayfair

The name says it all. Mayfair is posh London: the London of perfectly rounded vowels. I'm not sure where the name comes from but I presume it has something to do with the beauty of the surrounding parks in the month of May. Green Park, St James's Park and Hyde Park border Mayfair on three sides; the fourth border is delineated by Oxford Street.

Savile Row and Jermyn Street are in Mayfair, as are Bond Street's silversmiths, which is logical considering this is where most of the aristocracy, at the peak of the British empire, used to live. Life for the 'Mayfair set' was divided between riding in 'the park' (Hyde Park), sitting in the House of Lords at nearby Parliament and dressing for dinner. Tailors, bootmakers, shirtmakers and so on were an essential part of daily life and, as such, the best ones – most with royal warrants – ended up in Mayfair.

ARA
R K

E OPE   G THIS RENOVATION
R ON   STREET OR AROUND
              ARLE STREET

Gentlemen's clubs, solicitors' offices, grand residences and specialist shops made up the architectural signature of Mayfair, and in a way they still do. Admittedly in the age of electronic banking, a few stately bank buildings have been transformed into brasseries, and the solicitors have largely moved to the City, but some of the old guard survive.

Tailors like Gieves & Hawkes and bootmakers like John Lobb have reinvented themselves for a world in which one-off handmade is the ultimate luxury, but for those relegated to buying off-the-peg, Mayfair continues full-strength in the role of 'outfitter'. Today New Bond Street and Bond Street encompass just about every luxury brand known to global consumers, including a few English ones such as Asprey which have managed to stay unique to London. And, better still, the gentlemen's clubs now allow ladies.

brown's

Ever since the Great Fire of 1666, London has been steadily moving due west ... or, more accurately, London's wealth and status have been moving west. For a while Soho and Covent Garden housed the lion's share of the capital's dukes and earls but gradually, from the 1720s onwards, Mayfair became the city's most monied address, and so it has remained.

All the most expensive properties – the dark blue ones in the English version of Monopoly – are in Mayfair, and perhaps logically enough many of the city's finest hotels have followed. The Ritz, Claridges, the Dorchester and Brown's all ended up here. Famous, all, for their British grandeur and afternoon tea, as well as for their clientele, Brown's in particular has long been a favourite. Something to do, perhaps, with the Englishness of its wooden panelling and leather sofas, and for its status as an established watering hole for the area's Savile Row-clad gent.

In short, Brown's is an institution ... and institutions are tricky subjects for renovation. But they are exactly the kind of properties hotel entrepreneur Sir Rocco Forte is particularly good at taking on. Following successes with De Russie in Rome, the Amigo in Brussels and the Savoy in Florence, the Forte family have finally put their unique blend of chic modernity and old-fashioned service into play in their home market. And, once again, Forte's sister Olga Polizzi was responsible for the orchestration of the design and decoration.

The trick with renovating an institution is to do neither too much nor too little; to preserve what people have always loved while giving a fresh appeal. Although it was probably anything but simple to achieve, Polizzi chose a simple approach.

The bar is dedicated to the British photographer Terence Donovan and is decorated with his work. In The Grill, the hotel's elegantly pared-down restaurant, the distinctive wooden panelling remains but, through clever use of colour and white painted surfaces, the room is bright and sophisticated with a little twist of gent's-club ambience. In the guest rooms modernity dominates because, as Polizzi will tell you, she loves light, and considering the grey, dark winters of northern Europe it's a good thing.

The appeal of Brown's is based on detail sourced from an array of original and personal finds. From the specially commissioned lamps to the unusual door handles executed in pinkish-red glass, these are interiors for people who appreciate quiet but discerning taste. The locals who used Brown's as their watering hole have come back en masse, delighted with their institution's makeover. A cool classic is what we're all looking for.

address Brown's, Albemarle Street, London W1S 4BP
tel (44) (0)20 7493 6020   **fax** (44) (0)20 7493 9381
e-mail reservations.brownshotel@rfhotels.com
room rates from £350

absolutely have to see
Whatever is on at the Royal Academy, Burlington House, Piccadilly, London W1J 0BD (tel 7300 8000): a refreshingly diverse repertoire of exhibitions

must have lunch
The restaurant downstairs at Nicole Farhi, 158 New Bond Street, London W1S 2UB (tel 7499 8368): a casual classic in the Farhi flagship store

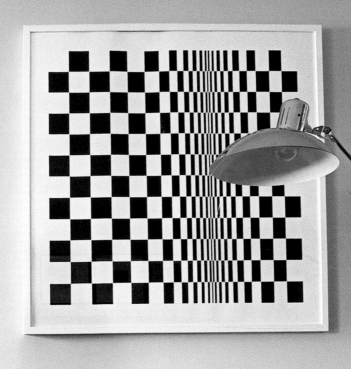

no. 5 maddox st

There is a new phenomenon in the world of hospitality that has recently begun to take on some momentum. Unfortunately it doesn't yet enjoy a name or title that is in sync with its attraction. The phenomenon is known as the 'aparthotel' – an awkward abbreviated combination of 'apartment' and 'hotel'.

The idea is straightforward. Not everyone visits for just a night or two, and if your stay is longer than a week you start to pine for more space and a greater measure of independence.

It was with this thought in mind that Tracy Lowy, the proprietor of No. 5 Maddox St, set up her Highly Individual Place, a collection of mini-apartments in the heart of Mayfair for the traveller who would prefer lots of space to lots of bellboys. No. 5 Maddox St caters to the visitor who either knows London or is prepared to discover it for themselves.

It is not, certainly, a hotel in the traditional sense. There's no lobby (unless you count the tiny front office, complete with groovy fish tank, open 24 hours a day), no restaurant (though a delivery service can be arranged), no public bar (though each kitchen has a bar or two of its own), no health club (though there are links to the one across the road) and no shopping arcade (though who needs one with New Bond Street around the corner?).

Guests stay here, often repeatedly, because they get an apartment like the kind of place they would live in in this city if they had the time, means and inclination to organize one for themselves … except in this apartment someone makes your bed, tops up your towels and cleans the kitchen and bathroom. It's possible not many guests actually use their kitchen, but it's nice to know they can if they want to.

In the end it's a lifestyle issue. Some of us love the 'yes sir, no sir, whatever you want sir' luxury of hotels; others find it tedious and tiring. Some like to have dinner in the comfort of their hotel dining room; others regard it as proof that you don't know where else to go. And, let's face it, if you know London as well as your concierge he becomes redundant. Being left to your own devices is not for everyone, but there are plenty of people that love the idea. All it needs now is a more user-friendly soundbite.

address No. 5 Maddox St, London W1S 2QD
tel (44) (0)20 7647 0200 **fax** (44) (0)20 7647 0300
e-mail no5maddoxst@living-rooms.co.uk
room rates from £250

absolutely have to see
The high-end stores on New Bond Street

must have lunch
Sketch, 9 Conduit Street, London W1S 2XG (tel 0870 777 4488):
Mourad Mazouz's over-the-top design fantasy set in a Georgian
mansion that houses an art gallery, two bars and two restaurants

soho

嘉麗華

Unlike New York's SoHo, which is an abbreviation of 'South of Houston', London's Soho was named for the hunting cry that could be heard before the area started to be built over in the 1600s.

Once one of the most upmarket addresses in London, Soho's reputation was built on anything but upstanding behaviour and good table manners. In almost every field, whether politics, music, multicultural ethnicity or pleasures of the flesh, Soho has been the venue for the more radical end of the scale.

Karl Marx lived here in exile, as did Rimbaud after the failure of the French Commune. Jazz found its first home here in smoky basement clubs, as did punk rock in the 1970s. And since the late 1700s Soho has held a reputation as London's venue for lively artistic watering holes –

starting with the Turk's Head in 1764, then the Colony Club in the 1950s, and the Groucho Club today – where writers and artists are able to bounce off each other's ideas. Soho is without a doubt one of the most colourful areas of London, with an edge and a taste for the wilder side of life, fuelled in part by a core of advertising and film production businesses on Wardour Street.

In keeping with its unorthodox profile it's no surprise that it's also the venue for the capital's Chinatown, complete with festive dragon gates at either end of Gerrard Street – a dense stretch of inexpensive and not-so-inexpensive chop shops specializing in anything from Peking to Sichuan to Cantonese cuisine. The earlier fascination for opium dens, as in Thomas De Quincey's book *Confessions of an Opium Eater* written in the early 1800s, may have subsided but Soho's Chinatown is still plenty exotic.

hazlitt's

Situated in an immaculate Georgian townhouse, on a small street just off Soho Square, Hazlitt's is a subtle but stylish piece of authentic London history.

Although much of Soho has been modernized with the arrival of small design-led businesses in advertising, public relations, graphic design and film and television production, and the accompanying lifestyle has seen an explosion in loft-living, the area still has the odd cobbled street with intact townhouses. The first impression, particularly for visitors to London, must be how small these look compared to their Victorian or Edwardian counterparts. It's true that they are hardly mansions, but their strength derives not from the glamour of big rooms or high ceilings, but from proportions that are personable and, just as important, pragmatic. With their raised and fielded panelling, their fireplaces and low ceilings, these houses would have been particularly cosy, as well as easy – and cost-efficient – to heat. They are a living testament to the Georgian skill at the art of proportions.

Nowhere is this more true than at Hazlitt's, a triple row of houses intelligently and sensitively converted into a hotel. Apart from the addition of modern plumbing, the spaces and proportions are just as they would have been, and that's the real appeal of staying here.

On another level, being here also provides insight into both London and Britain. While the French were living in grand apartments with impossibly high ceilings and ornate everything, the British were much more modest, living in smaller houses with simpler furniture. It's this restraint, coupled with historic authenticity, that provides such a vivid experience at Hazlitt's today.

William Hazlitt was a writer, critic of note and biographer of Napoleon in early nineteenth-century London. When he died in 1830 – in one of the three houses that comprise the hotel today – it was still then a boarding house. Inspired by Hazlitt's writing and his sensitive, distinctly non-stiff-upper-lip approach to life, Douglas Bain and Peter McKay set out to create an experience that would be a world away from the hustle and bustle of contemporary Soho. They named their creation after Hazlitt and imbued it with the same sentiment that he invested in his words. 'Grateful and contented' was the epitaph he requested for his tombstone. How surprised would he be to discover that they have in effect become a manifesto for a unique inner-city hotel.

address Hazlitt's, 6 Frith Street, Soho Square, London W1D 3JA
tel (44) (0)20 7434 1771 **fax** (44) (0)20 7439 1524
e-mail reservations@hazlitts.co.uk
room rates from £175

absolutely have to see
Foyles, 113–119 Charing Cross Road, London WC2H 0EB (tel 7437 5660): fossick around London's most eccentric bookstore for original first editions

must have lunch
Bar Italia, 22 Frith Street, London W1D 4RF (tel 7437 4520): the enduring and unchanged original London espresso bar, with the best toasted ciabatta in northern Europe

the soho hotel

Situated in the very heart of London's arty, bohemian Soho – an area ripe with private clubs, ethnic restaurants, Italian coffee bars and sex shops – is The Soho Hotel, the largest and, to date, hippest addition to Tim and Kit Kemp's stable of London hotels.

With two cinemas, a restaurant, several thematic bars and countless meeting rooms, as well as a monumental Botero sculpture in the reception, The Soho is a far cry from the small, club-like hotels that were the norm for this area. But the Kemps' gamble has paid off. Refuel Restaurant is consistently full, the bars and meeting rooms are continually booked out, the cinemas feature special screenings to which invitations are eagerly anticipated, and the hotel is often fully booked … which is understandable given that the Kemps' commitment to scale doesn't end with the rooms.

By London standards the guest rooms are huge and, perhaps just as importantly, they are flooded with daylight. Staying true to the local vernacular of loft-living, the rooms are vast rectangular spaces that feature a wall of floor-to-ceiling windows, opening onto narrow terraces. But counter to the loft cliché, the rooms are not pale and sparse. Instead they are brightly coloured and sumptuously furnished with big squishy couches and big works of art. These are rococo retreats, more in the style of Julian Schnabel's eclectic baroque loft, than the more predictable all-white art gallery space.

The Soho Hotel has seized on one significant fact: 'rock stars don't do minimal'. Even if you haven't watched every episode of MTV Cribs, it's clear that 'a bit of bling' is better than none at all. And most high-profile media personalities prefer their interior bling in a particular way.

Big sofas, big art, big flatscreen TVs and big splashes of colour are the new must-have ingredients of celebrity nesting – the interiors equivalent of diamond-encrusted jewelry and Tahitian tattoos – and The Soho has taken note. As a guest you get the oversized features but you also get them in a style that is still distinctively British. If there's such a thing as 'restrained bling', then The Soho Hotel can be credited with having invented it.

address The Soho Hotel, 4 Richmond Mews, London W1D 3DH
tel (44) (0)20 7559 3000 **fax** (44) (0)20 7559 3003
e-mail soho@firmdale.com
room rates from £240

absolutely have to see
James Smith & Sons Umbrellas, 53 New Oxford Street, London WC1A 1BL (tel 7836 4731): an extraordinary institution, where you can still have an umbrella made to your size while you wait

must have lunch or afternoon tea or dinner
Yauatcha, 15 Broadwick Street, London W1F 0DL (tel 7494 8888): a Chinese patisserie, teahouse and restaurant in a Richard Rogers building

covent garden

It's a name that conjures up distinctly aristocratic associations, and so it was meant to. Covent Garden was once London's first attempt at a purpose-built luxury enclave. In the early 1600s the Earl of Bedford commissioned the celebrated architect Inigo Jones to design London's first planned square, with a series of Palladian-style arcades defining its spacious internal courtyard. Attracted by its 'grand tour' architecture – a styling taken directly from Renaissance Italy – the rich and the aristocratic came flocking.

Jones's seductive piazza also attracted merchants, hawkers and grocers, and in no time at all Covent Garden was host to an ever-expanding fruit and veg market. Rotting cabbages and aristocratic sensibilities were, however, not an enduringly successful combination and thus began Covent Garden's decline into an area known by the early eighteenth century as 'the great square

of Venus'. Gambling dens, coffee houses and bawdy bars became the new tenants of the square and, in a cheeky nod to its classic Italianate signature, the piazza also became well known for its *bagnios*: a promisingly Continental name for Turkish baths that doubled as brothels.

The aristocracy had by this time moved west to Mayfair but they were not averse to returning by night. The rich and famous could be found in 'the Garden's' restaurants, enjoying turtle soup after an evening at the theatre. The ladies would go home by carriage while the gents frequented the infamous whorehouses of Russell Street (true to British literary tradition there was even a 'Who's Who' of local whores penned by a well-known writer).

Today town planners are looking at ways to restore the piazza to its former glory. With the recent renovation of the Opera House, the signs are that the area is returning to its grand roots.

one aldwych

Music in the pool, television while you shave, an in-house cinema for private screenings, fibre-optic lighting, politically correct vacuum plumbing that uses 75 per cent less water than conventional systems: Gordon Campbell Gray has created a unique hotel by considering details beyond the conventional – details that even grand hotels would consider extravagant.

A veteran hotelier, Campbell Gray learned a thing or two about the dreams and demands of the modern luxury customer when he set up a successful business in Long Island, the playground of the rich and famous, where his neighbours included Calvin Klein and Martha Stewart. Later, inspired by the Hôtel Montalembert in Paris, he made a luxury checklist of his own. At One Aldwych he was intent upon eliminating the chintz and paring down the plush, clearing out the claustrophobic clutter that has traditionally defined luxury. That is why the walls are white, the fabrics are plain and the decorative detail is limited to the odd bolt of colour in the rich tones of Jim Thompson Thai silk. There's not a tassel in sight.

The aim was to eliminate the 'dripping deluxeness' – to banish any hint of snobbery and instead contribute something of value to the guest experience. That is why the hotel recruited leading personal trainer Matt Roberts to manage the immaculate fitness centre, with its glamorous Bugatti-blue mosaic-tiled pool. And that is why Campbell Gray hired ex-Ritz Julian Jenkins as the executive chef for the mezzanine restaurant Indigo. There is also the more formal dining option of Axis, a dramatic double-height space with a 1920s feel, distinguished by a massive mural by English artist Richard Walker.

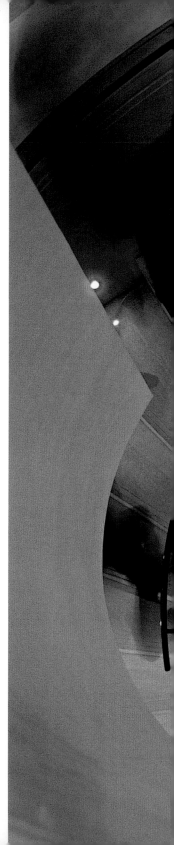

Even with all the details and services that have been pumped into this hotel, its most impressive element remains the architecture. This classically elegant corner building, originally built in 1907 as the offices of the *Morning Post*, is one of the most important Edwardian buildings in London. Its dignified Louis XVI-style stone exterior bears more than a passing resemblance to the Ritz – which makes sense given that it was designed by the same architects, Mewès and Davis, the Anglo-French partnership that was also responsible for the Paris Ritz.

Last but not least is One Aldwych's location. What still sets London apart from all other world cities is its vibrant theatre scene. In this respect, no hotel is better located. Most major venues, including the South Bank Centre, Shakespeare's Globe and the Royal Opera House, are within walking distance.

address One Aldwych, London WC2B 4RH
tel (44) (0)20 7300 1000 **fax** (44) (0)20 7300 1001
e-mail reservations@onealdwych.com
room rates from £185

absolutely have to see
National Portrait Gallery, St Martin's Place, London WC2H 0HE (tel 7312 2463): a uniquely British institution – a museum devoted to the emotive power of portraits, teamed with the odd contemporary photography exhibition

must have lunch
The gallery's Portrait Restaurant (tel 7312 2490): an inspired glass box on top of the new Ondaatje Wing; see a procession of London monuments at your feet

covent garden hotel

Situated in the very heart of Covent Garden, the hotel is a stone's throw from London's theatre world; a hop, skip and a jump from some of the city's most interesting boutiques, among them the original (and some say best) Paul Smith store in London; and a quick stroll from some well-established restaurants, including the Ivy. Then there's the ambience. As Australian-born head of public relations Craig Markham puts it, 'They're good at doing cosy.'

'They' are Tim and Kit Kemp, the husband-and-wife team behind several small, elegant hotels in the city (including The Soho Hotel). The design of Covent Garden's interior could never be considered cutting-edge contemporary, and nor does it try to be. What it delivers is a modern version of the classic British inn. It's all about curtains, carpets, fireplaces and tea – all the elements that go so well with London's often wet and grey weather. But don't imagine Covent Garden Hotel to be busy, twee or dated. Some of the rooms may have more than a hint of chintz, but the bathrooms are all gleaming polished granite with not a trace of the infamous plumbing for which London hotels used to be so notorious. In a nutshell, the look may be reassuringly old-style but the attitude is one hundred per cent up-to-date.

The hotel was designed to cater to individuals, and its guests are encouraged to find the room they most identify with. There's a room with a soaring ceiling height and mezzanine sleeping area; there are smaller, attic-style rooms dominated by four-poster beds; there's a mini-apartment that feels like a library with a sleeping annex; some rooms are feminine, some masculine; some are dark while others are filled with streaming daylight.

The restaurant, the bar and the upstairs guest salon are all a contemporary romantic version of the classic British gentleman's club interior for which London is renowned: oak panelling, lots of cosy wing chairs, big open fires. This, perhaps more than anything else, defines the modern London experience: a metropolitan multicultural mentality served in a setting that preserves a slightly old-fashioned style of intimacy without being fusty or retro. It's a delicate balance that London in general, and the Kemps in particular, are pretty good at.

address Covent Garden Hotel, 10 Monmouth Street, London WC2H 9HB
tel (44) (0)20 7806 1000 **fax** (44) (0)20 7806 1100
e-mail covent@firmdale.com
room rates from £220

absolutely have to see
Royal Opera House, Bow Street, Covent Garden, London WC2E 9DD (tel 7240 1200): glass masterpiece combining modern opera with classic architecture

must have dinner
Rules, 35 Maiden Lane, London WC2E 7LB (tel 7836 5314): traditional British food served in what is reputed to be London's oldest restaurant, opened by Thomas Rule in 1798

bloomsbury & fitzrovia

'Enough wood for 100 pigs' is how the Domesday Book describes this undomesticated area west of Old London and, until the late 1600s, it remained a wooded estate that belonged to a family of medieval landowners called the Blemunds – hence the name Bloomsbury.

After the Great Fire of 1666 there was a need for new building and in the late 1600s the Earl of Southampton built Bloomsbury Square – a noble piazza – in the west of the city. It established a trend for the area and many more of the formal squares that give Bloomsbury its distinct signature were built by the Dukes of Bedford who, through marriage, acquired most of the area. Perhaps appropriately the most handsome of all of these is Bedford Square, a perfect example of eighteenth-century architecture, all carefully symmetrical and uniform without being too grand.

Bloomsbury's Georgian style is a drawcard and the real star of the area is the British Museum, one of the world's great museums. Spread over two and a half miles of galleries, it houses one of the largest collections of antiquities (especially Greek and Roman art) in the world … not without some controversy as is the case with Lord Elgin's infamous 'Marbles', the Parthenon sculptures that the Greek government insists were stolen from their natural home.

With the close proximity of the museum as well as London University and the high-tech science museum of the Wellcome Trust, plus the fact that Charles Dickens used to live here, plus the fact that next door is Fitzrovia, the area that gained its name in the 1930s when writers and other artists began to gather at the Fitzroy Tavern, this part of London has acquired a well-founded reputation as London's most intellectual quarter.

myhotel bloomsbury

'Bloomsbury' was the name given to a bohemian movement – an arts and crafts revival – of early Edwardian England. At the time, the British Empire was at its peak and Britain was leading the world in mass-manufacture and industrialization. But a small group of artists, artisans and writers, which counted Duncan Grant, Roger Fry, Virginia Woolf and her sister Vanessa Bell among them, weren't convinced. Instead they proposed a return to traditional values in terms of artistic pursuit. The resulting ranges of textiles, pottery and furniture were indeed made by hand, but they were far from old-fashioned. Today, the legacy of Bloomsbury lives on in the appreciation of the products the group left behind, many of which are collected by museums.

Bloomsbury, the area, has developed a similar reputation for harbouring and nurturing creativity. Until recently it was the address for London's upper-end art and literary publishers, and its reputation for individual, against-the-grain thinking also made it an appropriate setting for London's avant-garde, break-all-the-rules architecture school, the Architectural Association. These days, highly inventive ad agencies have replaced the publishers but Bloomsbury's reputation for being a bit bohemian continues.

Which helps to set the context for myhotel. Stated quite simply, the area needed a hotel like this, and vice versa. The people who work locally have a popular bar to drop into after work or a place to meet for lunch, and the guests who work in advertising, etc. don't have far to walk for meetings. And in addition to the hotel's small dining bar, which opens onto the street in summer, there's a Yo! Sushi, the conveyor-belt, pay-for-what-you-take approach to Japanese 'hand food'.

Designwise, the hotel benefits from the same approach as myhotel Chelsea. And what does this mean exactly? Well, the interiors are an eclectic modernist mix while the ambience is one of distinctly British cosiness. It's an easy place to hang out, just as it's a comfortable place to stay. Perhaps myhotel Bloomsbury is a bit more cutting-edge than its counterpart in Chelsea but, given the area, that seems appropriate. Individual, small-scale, personalized and adventurously contemporary: the members of the Bloomsbury Group would be very proud of their legacy.

address myhotel Bloomsbury, 11–13 Bayley Street, Bedford Square, London WC1B 3HD
tel (44) (0)20 7667 6000 **fax** (44) (0)20 7667 6044
e-mail bloomsbury@myhotels.com
room rates from £230

absolutely have to see
The British Museum, Great Russell Street, London WC1B 3DG (tel 7323 8299): the place where all those colonial mementoes like the Elgin Marbles ended up; a surviving testament to Britain's once far-reaching empire

must have dinner
Busaba Eathai, 106–110 Wardour Street, W1F 0TS (tel 7255 8686): a new and attractive way to eat Thai, particularly in Christian Liaigre's all-teak interior

the sanderson

When it first opened a few years ago, the Sanderson generated a great deal of buzz. The ambience was that of a perpetual party: glammed-up people queued to get into the bar; the restaurant, Spoon, introduced a revolutionary deconstructed approach to eating (no starters or mains, just lots of dishes to share); and the all-white Agua Spa brought an urban feel-good factor to a grey, polluted metropolis. Chic sophistication was the name of the game.

But though locals and overseas visitors alike were clearly into the big white open spaces and the clever theatrical touches, the Sanderson wasn't very 'London'. Catered by a Frenchman (Alain Ducasse), designed by another Frenchman (Philippe Starck) and owned by an American (Ian Schrager), the hotel had no references to England's rich architectural past, nor to its various cultural institutions such as the pub, the cosy fireplace and afternoon tea. Even the location had nothing to do with tradition: this end of London's West End is home to the odd reinvented department store such as Selfridges, a handful of architectural kitchen boutiques, some very dodgy T-shirt shops and plenty of design studios, film production houses and cutting-edge ad agencies. The fact that there was really nothing 'British' about the hotel seems, however, to have been exactly what made it such a hit.

Guests who chose to stay here were making a conscious decision to avoid tradition. The big question was: would it last? The answer was, of course, yes. Today the bars are still packed, the spa is perpetually booked and Spoon is always full. What's the secret? Is it the triumph of style over cliché? Perhaps. But it's not as if Londoners are starved for choice.

I think there's an easier explanation for the hotel's success. And it's simply this. Staying at the Sanderson is a lot of fun. The food is great, the rooms are funky in a calm, soothing, all-white kind of way, there's plenty to do and, just as importantly, plenty to see in terms of people-watching. If you want British tradition, stick to Mayfair or Park Lane. If you want something different, reserve your spot now. And I defy any guest to walk straight to the elevator without stopping at one of the bars for a quick cocktail, or two, or....

address Sanderson, 50 Berners Street, London W1T 3NG
tel (44) (0)20 7300 1400 **fax** (44) (0)20 7300 1401
e-mail sanderson@morganshotelgroup.com
room rates from £295 inc. breakfast

absolutely have to see
Sir John Soane's Museum, 13 Lincoln's Inn Fields, London WC2A 3BP (tel 7405 2107): distinguished architect's house filled with architectural remnants

must have lunch or dinner
Hakkasan, 8 Hanway Place, London W1T 1HF (tel 7927 7000): Alan Yau's Michelin-starred establishment in an abandoned basement in the wrong end of town has reinvented the Chinese restaurant

clerkenwell

Sometimes referred to as the Soho of the East, Clerkenwell has recently seen a return of a residential population, which has, in turn, spurred a major revival in the area's fortune. All the former industrial buildings and mercantile warehouses have been converted into lofts, and the small shops that would once have housed tanners, bootmakers, glass-stainers and cheesemongers now showcase ethnic cuisine and brand-name espresso bars.

Four hundred years ago Clerkenwell was still a field, but as a result of the Great Fire of 1666 the area started to attract the homeless, and many people ended up staying. The fact that it was outside the jurisdiction of the City Corporation and free from the city's guild restrictions gave it additional appeal. It became a refuge for people unable to work in the city, particularly prostitutes. Indeed the area became famous for this, and Cock Lane today survives as a memento of the time!

With vice came crime and, teamed with a virtual population explosion between 1801 and 1861, Clerkenwell ended up becoming one of London's most densely inhabited – and unsalubrious – parts of town. In the centre was Smithfield Market, originally known as Smoothfield. It has been a site for trading livestock since 1173, and up until 1855 live cattle, sheep and pigs were still herded through the streets of Clerkenwell to market.

Flocks of sheep wandering through densely woven slums habituated by ladies of the night and all sorts of 'artful dodgers': it must have been quite a sight, not to mention an assault on the olfactory nerve. No wonder Dickens was inspired. And now that Clerkenwell has become an area of exuberant architecture and lively street life, where every other resident seems to be in film or design, the odd sushi bar seems very tame by comparison.

the zetter

The Zetter is right in the middle of London's Clerkenwell, and Clerkenwell is right in the heart of the 'new London'. It's the kind of area that has made the capital hip again. It's urban with a capital U.

This is definitely not the London of bobbies, doubledecker buses, black cabs and gents with rolled-up umbrellas. Nor is it the cosy pint-at-the-pub-after-the-football type of London. It's all lofts, converted warehouses and multi-ethnic bars, restaurants and cafés. Clerkenwell gives the impression of being inhabited only by designers, architects, funky ad agencies, creatives and whoever does whatever to warrant working and living in a loft. It's a bit like SoHo in New York, but without the black clothes.... And the loft thing is no exaggeration. Even the real estate agencies have nothing but loft spaces in their windows, the only variety being between warehouses converted into lofts and new-build loft-style apartments.

It was only a matter of time, then, before the area got a hotel in line with its ultra-urban street culture. The brainchild of Mark Sainsbury and Michael Benyan, the Zetter does a good job of fitting into the local scene. Its rooms are loft-like, its top-floor apartments even more so, and the restaurant – a vast warehouse-style space on the ground floor – serves up fusion cuisine prepared by a resident Australian chef (Aussies are credited with having started fusion). It's convincingly appropriate for Clerkenwell and, just as importantly, the prices have been kept as low-key as the area's ambience. In fact London's *Evening Standard* newspaper described the hotel as having 'the stylishness of Babington House at Holiday Inn prices'.

Where Sainsbury and Benyan deviated from the predictable was in the priorities they established, opting for cutting-edge technology over cutting-edge design. On each floor, swipe-card vending machines have replaced the antiquated mini-bar, and all the bedrooms are equipped with flatscreen televisions, a digital library of four thousand free music tracks and wireless Internet connection.

Stylewise, the approach could best be described as relaxed and comfortable in a dedicated-to-design kind of way (duck-down duvets and big-diameter rain-showers are standard). With its big spaces and laidback staff, the Zetter fits in perfectly with the ambience of this hip new London.

address The Zetter, St John's Square, 86–88 Clerkenwell Road, London EC1M 5RJ
tel (44) (0)20 7324 4444 **fax** (44) (0)20 7324 4445
e-mail info@thezetter.com
room rates from £140

absolutely have to see
Tate Modern, Bankside, London SE1 9TG (tel 7887 8000): not exactly next door, but worth the excursion

must have lunch
St John Bar & Restaurant Smithfield, 26 St John Street, London EC1M 4AY (tel 7251 0848): whitewashed former smokehouse with a fanatic following

the rookery

It's difficult to imagine in today's Clerkenwell of lofts, cutting-edge design and innovative fusion-style restaurants that this area was once one of the most risqué neighbourhoods of London. In the time of Dickens, it was positively Dickensian!

One odd bit of surviving Dickensian London, The Rookery, is completely convincing in its historic curiousness. Hidden away in a tiny cobblestone lane no wider than a donkey, it even retains the type of sign an inn of the 1800s would have had.

Once inside, the historic spell continues. Low ceilings, dark wood panelling, stone fireplaces and plenty of mahogany doors separating one small chamber from the next distinguish a set of interiors that could easily double as a set from the film version of Dickens's *Bleak House*.

The Rookery is a fantasy; the kind of folly you would only find in London. Yet, despite its historic ambience, it is nevertheless a fantasy of the funky variety. It's not surprising to discover that the proprietors are the same as Hazlitt's, the beautifully restored historic property in Soho. And to the advantage of the guest the hotel group has invested plenty of time and practice in perfecting their formula – a formula that emphasizes a very personalized hospitality, with carefully considered historic details: four-poster beds with heavy red velvet draught curtains from the eighteenth century, for instance, dominate the bedrooms, and most bath-rooms feature a freestanding claw-foot bath. In keeping with the notion of this being an individual experience, breakfast is only served on a tray in the room (let's face it, a buffet breakfast served in a breakfast room would completely destroy the historical web that has so successfully been woven here).

Cosy and club-like, the rooms at the Rookery are also romantically eccentric, and none more so than the Rook's Nest, the hotel's largest suite. With Victorian waterworks in one corner, an outrageous bed guarded by cherubic Moors in the other, and a cathedral-style living area/study upstairs, it ranks as one of the most photographed spaces in London. And, perhaps unintentionally, it refers back to Clerkenwell's historic reputation.

In the time of Dickens, Clerkenwell was London's centre of vice. So exotic and varied was the prostitution on offer that this area, located just outside London's official boundaries to avoid falling foul of the law, was famous all over Europe. Gradually London grew to encompass Clerkenwell and the brothels were closed down. Today Clerkenwell's vices are limited to those of the fattening variety, and of course the vicarious pleasure of experiencing Dickens's London.

address The Rookery, Cowcross Street, London EC1M 6DS
tel (44) (0)20 7336 0931   **fax** (44) (0)20 7336 0931
e-mail reservations@rookery.co.uk
room rates from £175

absolutely have to see
Shakespeare's Globe, 21 New Globe Walk, Bankside, London SE1 9DT
(tel 7902 1400): a working theatre, built as an authentic and faithful
reconstruction of one of the most famous playhouses of all time

must have lunch
Yo! Sushi, 95 Farringdon Road, London EC1R 3BT (tel 7841 0785):
a colour-coded conveyor-belt way to consume a memorable Japanese meal

Old London; the Square Mile; the Financial District. Defined by almost the same boundaries as the remnants of the walls from Roman times, the City is 'where London began'. Yet despite its 2,000-year-plus history, very little of this historic capital remains intact. More than three-quarters of it was wiped out by the Great Fire of 1666. Here and there, in the strangest places, you can still find the odd survivor of the fire's efficacy: the distinctively striped Tudor-style buildings built, precariously as it turned out, entirely in timber and stucco. They are rickety and uneven but characterful – testament to the folly of building in wood in close quarters … just as the spires of Sir Christopher Wren's cathedrals and churches, in particular St Paul's, remain as evidence of British backbone, despite the best attempts of the Luftwaffe to flatten them during the infamous Blitz of the Second World War.

The City is the strange, eclectic result of sweeping historic changes, but perhaps no change has had as much impact on its current incarnation as the effects of 1980s Thatcherite economics. Often without the prospect of sufficient numbers of corporate tenants, the City embarked on a building spree of unheard-of proportions. Glass and steel towers – some of exceptional daring and exquisite modernity – replaced the stone and brick of the previous Victorian building spree.

As in many global metropolises, London's City today has become a place to work, not to live. While more than 300,000 people spend a five-day week here, only 5,000 actually live in the Square Mile. The district remains the heartland of the nation's financial, legal, accounting and banking services, and it makes sense that some hoteliers have realized the potential of providing Highly Individual Places to stay in the City itself. After all, all work and no play makes....

great eastern hotel

Welcome to the sandwich-shop centre of the Western world! Until recently, the City of London offered little to match the urban sophistication for which the capital as a whole had earned a reputation. London's commercial heartland, a great world centre of the legal, banking and insurance industries, the City was something of a wasteland in terms of the finer things in life. Then along came Sir Terence Conran. In the late 1990s he acquired the grand Victorian railway hotel directly behind Liverpool Street Station and brought to it his West End magic. The result is a kind of contemporary lifestyle centre, not so different from the hugely successful Bibendum and Bluebird – only bigger. Much bigger.

Great Eastern is a giant. Besides the 267 bedrooms and suites – all different – the complex contains five restaurants and at least three bars (four if you include the exclusive members-only club). Fans of sushi and other Japanese fare can opt to dine in the slick contemporary interior of Miyabi, while enthusiasts of the more traditional British pub can get a (warm) beer and roast dinner in the Tudoresque surroundings of the George Bar. For more formal occasions or working lunches, which seem to have become much more popular since Great Eastern opened its doors, there is the Aurora Restaurant, a grand old space complete with leaded glass, a dome cupola and snooty waiters. Underneath huge modernist chandeliers constructed of overlapping flaps of paper, diners enjoy a menu that's billed as modern European cooking at its best. It's a spectacularly beautiful space that unfortunately is not as extraordinary as it would be if only it were populated by a few more women.

But the real plus, particularly for overseas visitors, is the hotel's splendid heritage. Liverpool Street Station, opened in 1875, was one of the great temples to the age of steam. When work began on the adjacent hotel shortly afterwards, provision was made for it to have its own tracks and sidings, not just for the convenience of the guests, but also for bringing in sea water for the hotel's sea baths. Travel then was for the very privileged, and the hotel architecture reflects the extravagant demands of its elite clientele. Corridors had to be wide enough for cabin trunks, and features such as the glass dome and main staircase had to be stupendously grand. In the process of renovation, these historic features were carefully preserved as modernity was intelligently inserted. With Great Eastern Hotel, Conran has really proved that you can breathe new life into a grand old girl.

address Great Eastern Hotel, Liverpool Street, London EC2M 7QN
tel (44) (0)20 7618 5000 **fax** (44) (0)20 7618 5001
e-mail reservations@great-eastern-hotel.co.uk
room rates from £225

absolutely have to see
St Paul's Cathedral; Sir Norman Foster's Millennium Bridge and his 'Gherkin' building at 30 St Mary Axe, London EC3; Sir Richard Rogers's Lloyd's Building on Lime Street, London EC3

must have lunch
The hotel's own Fishmarket restaurant (tel 7618 7200): grand hotel dining with a hip twist